We all Have Our Moments

Liz Cowley

GIBSON SQUARE

Also by Liz Cowley

Outside in My Dressing Gown (2014)
Gardening in Slippers (2015)

This edition published for the first time by Gibson Square

UK   Tel: +44 (0)20 7096 1100
US   Tel: +1 646 216 9813

info@gibsonsquare.com
www.gibsonsquare.com

ISBN   978-1-78334-100-9

Cover illustration by Dorrance.

Papers used by Gibson Square are natural, recyclable products made from wood grown in sustainable forests; inks used are vegetable based. Manufacturing conforms to ISO 14001, and is accredited to FSC and PEFC chain of custody schemes. Colour-printing is through a certified CarbonNeutral® company that offsets its CO2 emissions.

Printed and bound by CPI Group (UK) Ltd, Croydon, CR0 4YY

MOMENTS AT WORK

MOMENTS OF ANGER AND REGRET

MOMENTS OF RECKONING

MOMENTS OF DEPRESSION

AGE MOMENTS

FINAL MOMENTS

AXE

You stare in utter disbelief —
the hard drive's down, and yet again.
Just days ago you had it fixed —
not properly; that's all too plain.

And now you've got an urgent job.
You'll have to get it fixed today,
but then remember the repairer
was due to go on holiday.

He's now in Oz, in Adelaide —
a break he can afford to take.
You should have done a job like that —
my God, the money that they make!

How long's he off? You can't recall,
you'll have to get in someone new.
And what if they can't get it right,
and end up overcharging you?

You must be doing something wrong?
You're not, as far as you can see.
And what you once saw as a friend
is once again your enemy.

You long to take an axe to it,
and smash the wretched thing in two.
And now the hard drive's down again,
it won't be long before you do.

'IT'S SO EASY!'

Perhaps for *you* it may be easy.
That doesn't mean it is for me.
Why do people have to say that,
because they learn things easily?

Why do people have to say that
when teaching someone something new?
You may never ever say that,
but, sadly, lots of people do.

It's why I'm such a technophobe
and struggle to this very day.
'It's so *easy*!' Heard too often,
the worst thing anyone can say.

Immediately you feel a fool,
a clown, a dinosaur, a dunce,
and then withdraw inside yourself
and lose all confidence at once.

Too many times I've heard those words
when straggling, struggling way behind
with subjects I find hard to grasp –
not easy for my kind of mind.

The chances are that you have, too,
from someone, somewhere teaching you,
and may have given up like me
as far too many people do.

'It's so *easy*!' Not for some folk,
and sometimes, maybe, not for you.

Why do people have to say that,
and just because for *them* it's true?

A CHIPPED VASE

Of course I knew just what to do –
apply a drop of Superglue.
It looked so easy on TV.
But would the damned stuff work for me?

I glued the chip, two minutes passed –
by now it should have stuck, and fast –
then tapped the vase, the broken bit,
which promptly fell back into it.

'Patience, patience' then said I,
deciding on a second try,
and 'clink!' the chip fell in again –
another effort all in vain.

But third time lucky? Sometimes true,
but not with me and Superglue.
It wouldn't stick, the broken bit,
and now it wouldn't even fit.

Perhaps I'd put on too much glue?
It looked as if that could be true.
But scraping all of it away
would now take hours, perhaps all day.

Three attempts, and all in vain –
I simply didn't try again.
The vase was now an enemy,
the wretched thing had beaten me.

And mending it was such a bore,
I tossed it crossly on the floor,
and far from sitting there and crying
I found that truly satisfying.

The pieces scattered everywhere,
the vase now quite beyond repair.
How wonderful to hear it crashing;
revenge was absolutely smashing.

IN A CAFF

'Egg and bacon, please – no chips.'
'It always comes with chips as well.'
'I know. It doesn't have to, though.'
'It does in here – that's what we sell.'

'Of course I'll *pay* you for the chips.
Don't worry, I expected that.
I just don't want them on the plate,
you see, I'm cutting down on fat.'

'I'm sorry, have to serve all three,
that's what the staff are told to do.'
'I can't believe I'm hearing right!
I've hardly asked that much of you!'

'If *everyone* wants different things…'
'It isn't everyone, it's *me*.
And surely serving up two things
is easier than serving three?'

'I'm sorry Madam, rules are rules.
We can't change things, and just for you.
Please leave what you don't want to eat –
we find that's what most people do.'

'Okay, then bring a second plate –
I'll dump the bloody chips on that.'
'I'm sorry, but that's not allowed.'
'Well then, I'll use this plastic mat.'

'Use the mat? That's quite revolting!
You'll cover it with nasty fat.
I've never heard of such a thing.
How could you even *think* of that?'

'Okay, you win, then bring the chips.
I'll chuck them in that rubbish bin.'
'I'm sorry, that's against the law.
It's not for putting food waste in.'

I guess some rules are sensible,
but far too many others aren't.
Perhaps you just put up with them.
At times I find I simply can't.

FORGIVE ME!

I plan a busy day alone –
not half of it upon the phone.
'Just one more thing before I go!'
But is it *one* thing? Firmly, no!

'Guess what? I've joined the cricket club –
much nicer chaps than in the pub!
And one of them is such a hoot,
and in his whites he looks so cute!
I've found out he's a plumber too –
must get him round, there's loads to do!
The central heating's down again –
the bloody thing is *such* a pain:
Must let you go – I'm banging on.
Just one more thing, and then I'm gone!
Well, guess who I saw yesterday?
The chap I met on holiday,
you know, the one in Sicily
who fell a bit in love with me.
Oh, gosh – I'm banging on again,
I'm sorry to be such a pain.
Just *one* more thing before I go.
You know that woman down our street–
the one I said you'd like to meet?
She's turned out to be such a bore.
I can't think what I liked her for.
She's always here or on the phone.
She simply won't leave me alone.
Just one *last* thing before I go.'

It won't be *one* last thing – I know.
Just one? No, two or three or four,

and on occasions, even more.
At times, I stare at the receiver
and absolutely can't believe her.

'Just one more thing before I go!'
Why ever do I love her so?

SSSSHHH!

We watch the play, she's talked all day,
and now she makes a night of it.
She whispers to me all the time –
throughout the latest West End hit.
I put my finger to my lips, and pat her lap – to no avail.
But can I shut my girlfriend up?
Each time I try, I promptly fail.

She whispers to me all way through.
I've no idea what's going on,
and by Act Two I've lost the plot,
last scraps of concentration gone.
However much you love a friend,
there may be things you cannot share.
Of course, it's just the same for them,
with faults in *you* they cannot bear.

We soon forget the other's faults,
or else we hope they've changed a bit,
and then discover that's not true –
in fact, it's just the opposite.
We watched the play (or half of it)

and found a pleasant place to dine.
And still I love her as before –
forgiven, a great friend of mine.

TIME TO KILL

You're almost at the checkout,
one customer away –
you need to get through quickly –
you haven't got all day.

The woman who's before you
has loads of time to shop –
you know, because she's chatting.
Christ, will she ever stop?

She now can't find her glasses.
Can things get any worse?
Oh yes, you could have guessed it –
she's also lost her purse.

At last she finds her glasses –
of course, upon her head,
but not before you've offered
to lend her yours instead.

Thank God, she's found the money –
the whole thing takes an age.
By now, you're getting dangerous,
towards the murder stage.

A credit card? Forget it.
She's settling up in cash,
and counting it at snail's pace
just when you need to dash.

You cough, you start to fidget,
you even stamp your feet.
Now what's the woman up to?
She's checking her receipt!

You're normally good-natured,
but people at the till
who cannot move through smoothly
can make you want to kill.

'FANCY JOINING US AT THE PUB?'

Now Pete's on his iPad, and Bob's on his Blackberry,
and Don's on his iPhone, engrossed in a call,
while I sit there silent while watching them texting.
So why did I bother to come here at all?

Johnny is surfing around for red trousers,
while Willie and Heather are egging him on.
'Look at John Lewis, or Harrods may have them.'
'Blast, they *did* stock them, but now they've all gone.'

And Woody's no better, he's texting to Texas,
while Charlie is telling him what he should say.
'Ask for more info on things that you don't know,
and don't simply go there because of the pay.'

And Katy – not one word; engrossed in a crossword.
She can't get the name of 'an eye-opening drug'.
I know – Belladonna – but don't try and tell her.
She asks me; I answer, but just with a shrug.

And Prue's on her Samsung, finding a flight time,
and looking up prices of different air fares,
and Christopher, meanwhile, is glued to his mobile
(probably checking the state of his shares).

And Susan is late; her computer is crashing,
while Barry's upgrading his latest machine.
And now I've spilt wine across Peter's new iPad,
and he's livid, of course, as he can't read the screen.

I start to mop it, he tells me to stop it.
'Look, why don't you go and get us a drink?'
Technology – friendly? In private it may be.
In public, it's very *un*friendly I think.

ONE THING I'LL NEVER DO IN A BEDROOM

Have cushions scattered on the bed?
No. Frankly, that is not for me.
Take them off – and every evening?
How very tiresome that must be!

Then put them back again next morning –
in neat diagonals, each one?
I know a lot of people do.
But me? I wouldn't find that fun.

And who on earth will ever see them?
You two? The daily? Who else, pray!
And don't you find it so frustrating
replacing them, and every day?

I also find it truly maddening
to go to bed in B and Bs,
and find a load of cushions there.
I'm booked with you? No cushions, please!

Why put a row of cushions there?
They'll only land up on the floor
and have to be replaced at dawn –
and that's a waste of time, a bore.

Why bother with a load of cushions?
Why give yourself another chore?
Cushions are for sitting rooms.
On beds – whatever are they for?

Or maybe I am missing something,
Although I truly can't think what.
To prop you up? That *can't* be true.
At least, I truly hope it's not!

WHY DO WE PUT UP WITH IT?

Embrace your neighbours in a church?
That's simply not the British way.
Who introduced that sort of thing

and made us long for yesterday?

'Can I help you?' That was nice
when wandering around a store.
But now they say '*How* may I help you?'
and answering becomes a bore.

You know why they are saying that –
you can't reply with 'Yes' or 'No'
the way we always used to do
when going shopping years ago.

Sales teams phoning me from Mumbai
researching a consumer trend,
who talk as if they're mates of mine –
that also drives me round the bend.

Two kisses now – I don't mind that,
but loads of other people do,
especially when leaving folk
they've only known an hour or two.

People plugged into their Walkmans
who do not hear or see your car.
One day I'll run someone over.
How dangerous those gizmos are!

'Good morning!' Pleasant, lovely greeting,
but not when people add 'to you',
and these days on the radio,
presenters almost always do.

Perhaps, alas, I'm getting stuffy,
but all the same it's so frustrating

to find things changing all the time,
or else becoming irritating.

Pet hate? People on their mobiles
when at a meal – oh, that I hate,
especially if I have cooked it
and only just served up their plate.

GOSSIP

'Gossip, gossip, gossip, gossip –
why *can't* you women get enough?
Just look at all those magazines –
How can you bear to read such stuff?

What news so glues you to celebs –
and often minor ones at that?
Who needs to know their latest fads,
or what they've called their dog or cat?

Who cares who's had a nip and tuck,
or which one's made a fashion gaffe –
and turned up at the Oscars' night
in something hideously naff?

Who cares which one has given birth
or who designed the christening hat,
or how they've had the nursery done?
Whoever wants to know all that?

And who minds what they eat (or not),

and what their latest diet is?
Just why do women love all that?
Why *do* you love celebrities?

'Gossip, gossip, gossip, gossip –
I've never ever met a man
who laps up magazines like that
as avidly as you lot can!'

THE WORD 'UNI'

'Uni' – what a ghastly word.
Much better, 'university'.
Small wonder now that most of us
treat students less respectfully.

The truth is, 'uni' sounds too flip.
We picture fun, but not degrees,
or if we do, we think of ones
that won't be worth the student fees.

'Uni' sends the wrong impression –
it sounds like anyone can go.
Too populist, and far too pat
for loads of people whom I know.

So often I've heard people say
they find the name change irritating;
employers too, which can't bode well
for all the graduates in waiting.

It's tough enough to get a job,
and getting worse it seems to me
since 'uni' landed on the scene
instead of 'university'.

The moment we decide to change things
can take things backwards – to our cost,
and 'uni' is a fine example
of when respect was largely lost.

FAIRY LIQUID

How could she mention washing up
while looking at a gorgeous view?
A lovely spot in the Cevennes –
all mountains, rivers, skies of blue.

'I've never ever switched from Fairy.
I think you ought to use it too.
Why don't you bring some over here?
I know I would, if I were you!

It lasts for ages, really does.
For me, at least a month or two.
And what the advertising says
is, just for once, completely true!

You only need a single squeeze,
with other stuff, it's two or three.
Quite probably they sell it here –
I tell you what, I'll go and see!

I'm sure the French have heard of it –
I think it's famous everywhere.
You know your local Super-U?
I'm certain that I'll find it there!

If not, I'd bring a suitcase load.
It's worth the charge you'd have to pay.
Well, think of all the washing up
you have to do on holiday!'

Of course, she'll come to stay again –
she's always here a week or two,
but won't show her that spot again
where Fairy Liquid spoiled the view.

And if I ever go alone,
it never will be quite the same.
I'll always think of Fairy now.
I know I will, and what a shame!

THE CARPENTER'S SHOP

'Let's go inside, my darling –
that table's heavenly.
Not often that you see that –
such skills in carpentry!'

'Oh, Christ, it's too expensive!'

'It's not, my price is fair.

And Madam, it's not pleasant
to hear a lady swear.

Of course it's quite expensive.
It's olive wood, that's why.
That's very hard to work with.
Most carpenters don't try.

It took two months to make it,
I know the price is fair.
The cedar one is cheaper –
the one just over there.

I have to earn my living,
we carpenters all do,
although the world forgets that.
If only people knew.

It's worse for me – I'm Jesus.
You know, the son of God.
They can't believe I'm earning.
Most people find that odd.'

'Oh Jesus, goodness heavens!
Good Lord, I never knew.
You have to earn a living?'

'Oh yes, of course I do.'

AT A CHARITY BALL

Here sit I, by a banker chap
whose words hold no surprises.
And worse, his hand's been on my lap
right through the raffle prizes.

He's won it! Gosh, the holiday –
two weeks out in Bermuda.
'Do come with me!' I hear him say.
I could have been much ruder.

I wish the chap would shut his trap,
his words are so, so, boring,
and if he doesn't cut the crap,
I think I'll soon start snoring.

The problem with most balls like this
is all the balls you're hearing
from strangers sitting next to you,
who sometimes aren't endearing.

AT A DINNER PARTY

We sorted out the whole of Europe,
and did just that in three hours flat.
Alas, if only politicians
could do a little more of that!

And then, content, we drove off home,
collapsing happily in bed,

and then forgot just how we'd done it,
and every word of what we'd said.

Frustrating that we can't recall
our brilliant European plan.
Does any guest remember it?
I'm pretty sure that no-one can.

Moments in Love

'TO FALL IN LOVE'

'To fall in love' – an odd expression,
as if we've stumbled into it.
Anyone who's been in love
will know it's not like that a bit.

In love, we climb, we soar, we fly,
and none of us 'falls' into it
as if we're on a downward slope.
In fact, it's just the opposite.

And 'fall' suggests we may be hurt.
And that, of course, is often true –
but only when we're falling out
and splitting up, as couples do.

And 'fall' in any other sense
is negative, or not that nice.
The only time we like a fall
is when we see a fall in price.

'Head over heels' – that's also odd,
as if we've smashed our faces in.
In fact, we're running on a high
and coursing with adrenaline.

I guess we're stuck with some expressions.
They're ancient – and they're here to stay.
And 'fall in love' is one of them;
there's simply nothing else to say.

MISMATCH

'The trouble with our cruisers...'

'I knew a sailor once!'

'I sometimes think, my darling,
I'm married to a dunce.
I'm *sure* you knew a sailor.
Most people did or do.
Why is it with my stories,
you bring things back to you?
The trouble with our cruisers –
the strategy was flawed ...'

'A lovely chap! A young cadet.
I fell quite overboard!'

'Christ! *Will* you stop digressing?
It makes you sound so stupid!'

'And I've still got his Valentine.
He tried to draw a Cupid!'

'In Jutland, Admiral Beatty
lost thousands in one day...'

'His uniform was smashing
the day he sailed away!
His buttons were quite dazzling,
all glinting in the sun!
I took a load of photos
and framed the nicest one!'

'Why *is* it with *all* stories
you bring things back to you?'

'It's only when *you're* boring,
and then of course I do!'

THE MOMENT SHE TOLD YOU

Your best friend's fallen for your neighbour.
You love her – and her husband too.
You've known them both for years and years,
and now you don't know what to do.

You introduced her to her lover –
your fault that it has come to this.
She's phoning you, but what to do?
Not picking up is cowardice.

Support her? Lose her husband's friendship?
Stay neutral? Don't take any sides?
Keep out of it, don't speak of it,
until such time as she decides?

Don't phone, in case her husband answers?
Just wait, and then let time decide?
Keep talking, but keep off the subject,
or hear her out, let her confide?

Point out a fault the new man has –
a fault that she may not have seen?
Point out, at times we all look back

and dream of what life could have been?

Remind her of her husband's strengths
and all the things she stands to lose?
Remind her, when we're getting on,
to start again is not good news?

Resort to all those time-worn clichés?
'Oh, darling, this could end in tears.
Of *course*, the new chap's more romantic –
you haven't lived with him for years!'

Remind her that no man is perfect?
Again, remind her of her age?
Point out that if she leaves her chap,
she could regret it at some stage?

Remind her of the vast upheaval –
the house, the pictures, furniture?
(You've stayed with them, and countless times,
you know how much they mean to her).

Point out the new man's penniless,
and say that love can't conquer all?
And tell her that 'til she decides
you cannot get involved at all?

And tell her she can't come to stay
and then go round to see her lover?
And make it clear you're not prepared
to act as go-between and cover?

Or tell her you'll be there for her
whatever she decides to do,

(while knowing in your heart of hearts
that may not be entirely true)?

A nightmare if you love them both
(and rather like the new man too).
Keep out of it? That's bloody hard.
You can't. But what else can you do?

THE MOMENT YOU MET

Your life has turned a corner.
Why? Last week, so did you –
the very moment he did,
when bumping into you.

He was rushing somewhere,
with someone else to meet.
He almost knocked you flying.
You stayed – just – on your feet.

'Are you okay?' he asked you.
You laughed. 'I'm fine!' you said.
And now, a few weeks later,
he's upstairs in your bed.

So often on love's journey,
we reach a cul-de-sac,
and then we turn a corner,
and things are back on track.

You're firmly round that corner.

No reason now to mope.
As best friends always told you
'Don't ever give up hope.'

TO FLEE OR NOT TO FLEE?

To leave, or not to leave: that is the question.
Whether 'tis nobler for a wife to suffer
the slings and arrows of a husband's outbursts,
or to take arms against a sea of grumbles,
and by our exit, end them? To flee, to fight
no more, and by our leave to know we end
the heartache and the constant daily moans
we now put up with. That's a tough, tough question
that needs my answer soon, or even now.
What wife can bear the scorns and whips of time,
the oppressor's wrong, the husband's slurs
and constant bickering? To leave, to go,
to start once more, to dream – aye, there's the chance.
For in my current state, what dreams are there?
Why wait until I've shed this mortal coil?
But I must pause, since marriage is a vow –
a promise I would stay, and stay for life.
Divorce – what hell is that? The law's delay,
the misery of telling children, friends,
dividing up the spoils, the loneliness,
perhaps, alas, regretting it one day.
So, flight or fight? What best to do in life?
Ah, sometimes what it is to be a wife!
Security makes cowards of us all,
and makes us rather bear the ills we have

than fly to others that we know not of.
And thus I will remain within my cage
with sorrow and regret until old age
unless I find the bravery to flee,
but will I? No, and that's the tragedy.
I've lost the name of action, that is why,
and no longer have the courage now to fly
though love has all but ended.

Rhythm from 'To be or not to be' by William Shakespeare

LISTENING TO A FRIEND

'I watched him talk all evening –
about himself of course,
and suddenly it hit me:
I wanted a divorce.

For ages I had managed
to somehow carry on,
and suddenly I pictured
myself when he had gone.

A life ahead without him,
the person I could be,
and what I could be doing
if only I were free.

No longer was I listening
to anything he said,
the only voice I heard there
was mine, within my head.

'Get out, and soon!' it told me,
and did so loud and clear.
I thought I had to tell you,
and that is why I'm here.

It's good of you to see me.
I hoped I'd find you in.
And yes, I'll take your offer –
I'd love a good stiff gin!'

MEETING A NEW CHAP

Two marriages – and both behind him.
You vaguely wonder what went wrong,
especially if you then discover
that neither of them lasted long.

Three marriages? Mmm, that's disturbing.
And four? That's one too much for me.
There must be something very wrong.
Stop flirting please, and leave me be!

A MOMENT AT THE CHRISTMAS TREE

He helped me with the Christmas tree
while standing very close to me –
a man I'd met a month before
and clicked with almost instantly.

Two kids and married – that I knew,
but not, it seemed that happily,
or why would he drop in like that,
and also without telling me?

I'd never told him my address,
but didn't mind that someone had –
delighted that he'd called on me.
The truth was, I was more than glad.

I'd told him that I was divorced,
and noticed he was drawn to me,
exactly as I was to him –
the tension crackled round that tree.

And what a bloody fool I was.
What utter, sheer stupidity
embarking on a love affair
that never could end happily!

It didn't last – well, only months,
the guilt too much for him and me,
but every year I think of him
when putting up my Christmas tree.

I look at all the fairy lights –
the Christmas star he placed on top
recalling when I saw him last
and when we knew it had to stop.

A married man – solicitor,
and now a distant memory,
remembered only once a year
when putting up the Christmas tree.

SUDDENLY IN A CATHEDRAL

She walked the endless nave alone
and marvelled at the architecture.
She stroked the pillar, felt its cold,
and gazed upon its marble texture.

The altar beckoned, she moved on –
too late to make another prayer,
but just to stand where candles shone
and incense floated in the air.

She pictured him just down the road,
and in an internet café –
the places where he always spent
three quarters of each holiday.

No matter when or where they went,
the office took priority.
The countless times she'd told herself
'He never makes the time for me.'

Now, at the altar, all alone,
quite suddenly she knew they'd split.
She'd had enough of second place.
and knew that was the end of it.

That last day on their holiday,
while listening to a soothing hymn,
was when she knew she'd had enough
and finally was leaving him.

Moments in Marriages

TOO MUCH PLANNING

The organ starts,
and I take my first slow steps up the nave
dragging doubts and swathes of silk in my wake,
centre stage in a pantomime,
the lead part in the last act
of singledom.

A flurry of feathered hats
floats in my direction.
The congregation smiles me ever onwards
as my father guides me to my fate,
now thirty feet away.

Six weeks of doubting,
drowned out by fretting and flapping
and planning and primping
and pinning and presents.
'Don't worry, darling, it's only last minute nerves!'

I notice my aunt in the front pew
and remember the wine cooler she gave us.
Why do you need a wine cooler if you have a fridge?
And it has room for only one bottle.
And you have to clean it out every time you use it.
And it has a plug, so you can't even take it on picnics.
This is madness:
I'm almost there, and I'm thinking about wine coolers.

The organ stops.
The silence is suffocating, closing in.
The vicar takes my hand.
It's too late now.

THE MOMENT SHE CHANGED

She's changed, gone to another planet.

She speaks differently,
in soft, sentimental coos.

Dinners aren't what they used to be.
Nor is anything.

Nights are long and lonely –
she is always too tired.

Her eyes are elsewhere,
her ears are elsewhere.

There is someone else in her life.

A baby.

RECIPE

Take a woman and a man –
sprinkle her liberally with rose petals, blossoms of jasmine,
and fine French wine.
(Champagne may also be used).

To him, add spices, sauce and red-hot pepper.
Whisk constantly.
Blend until smooth; there should be no lumps.
Allow to bubble for two years at maximum heat –

the top should be frothy with golden peaks.

Add a baby, and stir.

Gradually remove all other ingredients, and
simmer at low temperature for a further two years.

Allow to cool.

Now, take a sharp knife and slice in two.

SEPARATE MOMENTS

At times, it's nice in marriages
to go your separate ways.
The moments we most often do
is on museum days.

I tend to look at human things –
what people ate and wore,
and how they lived and worked and died,
(or simply coped if poor).

My husband looks at maps and charts
and model boats and things,
and never can resist a tank
or anything with wings.

I look at wartime relics too,
but less so armoured ones.
I'd rather look at photographs,

LIZ COWLEY

or letters from lost sons.

He looks at anything that moves,
he's mad about machines –
while I am into portraits more,
especially family scenes.

Room sets, antiques, furniture –
he's not as keen as me,
but give him rooms of dinosaurs,
he's happy as can be!

At times it's great in marriages
to split up now and then,
and celebrate the differences
we often have from men.

MOMENTS IN BED

I wish she would come a bit faster.
I wish he would slow down a touch.
I wish she'd do things that are different.
I don't like the different things much.
I wish that she didn't like reading,
or at least not like reading in bed.
I wish he would not slap my book shut,
expecting some action instead.
I wish that we had the same sex drive.
I wish that we did, I agree.
I wish she'd do more things that *I* like.
I wish he would think more of me.

I wish we did not have a telly.
In bedrooms, the wrong place to be.
I wish he would just watch the programme,
and while it is on, leave me be.
I wish she would not wear a nightdress;
I wish she would listen to me.
I wish he would buy some pyjamas,
but know that he'll never agree.
I wish that she'd like more adventure.
I wish that he'd like rather less.
But I love her, I have to admit that.
But I love him, I have to confess.

THE CURSE OF CAPABILITY

The trouble, if you're 'capable'—
you don't get fancy things.
You're given a new casserole,
but never diamond rings.

The more you do, the less men do
in matters of the heart.
That soft embrace or single rose –
they soon forget the art.

'You're good at that,' they say to you.
You *are* – so carry on –
until the day it dawns on you
the spark has somehow gone.

The trouble, if you're 'capable',

you watch while other wives
who cannot do a bloody thing
lead more romantic lives.

'My husband has just bought me this!'
They twirl, in some new dress,
while showing me a Prada bag.
It irks, I must confess.

And if you also earn your keep,
well, then it's even worse.
You'll dine out yes, but only Dutch,
he'll empty half your purse.

The more we do, the less they do
in matters of the heart.
The answer is to do much less,
and do that from the start.

DANGER

Support, respect, encouragement,
and praise at times for what we do
should help to keep the boat afloat,
and bobbing rather nicely too,
but only if it's mutual;
it has to be a two-way thing.
And if those moments aren't returned,
their absence threatens everything.

Support, respect, encouragement,

and praise for what we do or think –
with that we thrive, but not without;
in time we find our spirits sink.
And then resentment climbs on board,
and once it's there, it tends to grow.
Its habit is to take the helm,
and then the problems truly show.

Now, all at sea, we talk much less,
go out more often on our own,
or else we wish our partners would,
and simply leave us time alone.
And then, if things are not resolved,
there comes a point we're more like strangers,
and thrashing round within ourselves,
we're open to all sorts of dangers.

The worst one is, when seeking solace,
we very often find it too,
when vulnerable, our judgement shot,
and meeting up with someone new.
They flatter us, they give us praise,
they're interested, supportive too.
We can't see they're quite wrong for us,
'til much too late – and then we do.

A SECOND MARRIAGE

The beauty of a second marriage –
you've learned what can go wrong before,
and what can screw a marriage up

and send it to the exit door.

The beauty of a second chance
to get it right as someone's wife
could be that he, not only you,
has learned a little bit in life.

The beauty of another try
to find contentment, get it right,
is finding out it's far, far more
than what you choose to do at night.

ADVICE IN A 1960S WOMEN'S MAGAZINE

(absolutely genuine, though reproduced in verse)

'Before your husband's back from work,
be sure it's tidy everywhere.
And wear a pretty floral dress,
and tie a bow upon your hair!

No toys around the carpets, please!
And also, no vexatious noise.
The poor chap's been at work all day.
No rowdy little girls and boys!

Don't prattle! He won't want to hear
you've cleaned the oven, done the chores,
and even found the time to shop
and tidy up and brush the floors.

And *always* have his dinner ready,

with meat, two veg – and piping hot.
He's worked all day, keep that in mind,
while you have not achieved a lot!

And when it's time to go to bed,
Forget your needs, remember his.
And watch out for next month's advice
on what a happy marriage is!

Above all, readers, do remember
he's more important than you are!
Remember all he's paying for:
the children, you, the house, the car.

Your needs are secondary to his.
Remember that, please, every wife.
And that's the very best advice
you'll ever have in married life!

(ℱe)male Moments

'THAT'S NOT HOW *I*'D HAVE DONE IT'

'Mmm, that's not how *I*'d have done it.'
'I'm sure it isn't. I'm not you.'
'No, and I'd have done it better.
Look! Surely you can see that's true!'

'Perhaps. The fact is, that it's *done*.'
'And very poorly in my view.'
'Too bad. At least I've mended it.
I'm sick and tired of asking *you*.'

'Yes, but I'd have done it *right*.'
'Perhaps, but I just couldn't wait.
And waiting ages, weeks or months,
is something that you know I hate.'

'So now you'll have to look at it,
and mended quite appallingly.
Why can't you ever understand
some jobs are better left to me?'

THE ROMANTIC

Last week we went to the sea.
Waves with frothy edges of whipped cream
dissolving into Victorian lace and windblown granny curls.
And all underfoot was shining beach jewellery,
sea-sucked pebbles licked into smooth boiled sweets.
The sand was pocked and pimpled by raindrops,
and I wrote our names there –

sloping,
slanting,
for the sea to steal and swallow.

And you skimmed a pebble
and said you felt like breakfast.

This week we went to the country.
I looked at fields kissed in mist,
skybankwater knit in grey wool.
An army of shining blades glittered at our feet.
Gossamer sacs cradled dewdrops.
I looked at spiked conker cases littering the path
robbed of their inmates by laughing children,
at russet rotting apples lying on lawns,
mildew-fluffed fruit, oozing juice,
at naked trees sighing and leaves flying.

And you looked at your watch.

WHY CAN'T *YOU* DO IT?

'Why can't you e-mail notes of thanks
or send a friend a letter?
Why *is* it always left to me?

'You do it so much better!'

'Why *is* it always left to me
to buy a gift or card?'

'It's really very simple, dear –
you don't find it as hard.'

'What rubbish! It's a selfish streak
to leave it to your wife.
You'd have to do that sort of thing
if I weren't in your life.'

'I wouldn't. I'd find someone else
to do the things you do.'

'I'm sure you would. That's no surprise.
I *quite* believe that's true!'

'I WISH THAT YOU WOULD SOMETIMES....'

'I wish that you would sometimes make the bed.
I wish you'd sometimes iron, or cook or clean.
or do some other household task instead,
and wouldn't tell me 'That is not my scene.'
I wish that you would sometimes use your brain
and notice when the basin's full of scum,
and wouldn't always say when I complain
'Why bother when the daily's due to come?'
But if I left as much of it to you,
I know that everything would go to pot.
I'm sick and tired of asking you, that's true,
but tell myself I still love you a lot.
You have your faults, I guess I also do,
but still, those faults don't stop me loving you.

Metre from Sonnet LXXI, William Shakespeare

CHRISTMAS PRESENTS

Why is it most men can't wrap presents
as artfully as women do?
Of course, some do – but very few.
I've often noticed that. Have you?

Why is it men can't wrap things well?
I've rarely met a chap who can.
It often seems that wrapping things
is quite beyond the wit of man.

What's stranger still is when a man
has quite an eye for geometry,
except when wrapping up a gift –
that's yet another mystery.

Most struggle with the wrapping paper
and how to get the angles neat,
and rarely bother with a ribbon
to make it look a special treat.

Few men, I think, can wrap a gift
as artfully as women do,
or else, they make that their excuse
for leaving wrapping gifts to you.

WHEN MEN ARE ILL

When men are ill, they take each pill
as if they're on the point of dying.

They seem to have a special skill
of groaning, moaning, choking, sighing.
'I wonder what it is,' they'll say.
'It's so much worse than yesterday.'
'It's nothing' say frustrated spouses,
fed up with witnessing their houses
set up with every sort of pill
to rectify some minor ill.
At which point men become more terse,
and end up feeling even worse.
The fact that women, tougher stuff,
take minor ailments on the cuff
is lost upon their sea of ills
and even greater sea of pills.

CONTROL FREAK

A man who always has to win
is not the one to share your life –
unless you want to ruin it.
What agony, if you're his wife!

If simple day-to-day decisions
can never be discussed in calm
and you are always giving in,
then that should ring a big alarm.

Temper's wearing, makes all sharing
impossible, or hard to do.
And if it's coupled with controlling,
then I'd take stock if I were you.

Hang in there? Then the time may come
you're beaten into weak submission,
without the strength to stand your ground
(which, probably, is his ambition).

Most people are surprised that anger
is listed as a deadly sin.
You wouldn't, with an angry man
who always, always has to win.

The time comes when you're going out
a lot more than you used to do,
alone, to have a quiet life,
and stop him from upsetting you.

If your man can't discuss things calmly
and has to shout and scream at you,
and you can't change him (or yourself)
it's pretty clear you're doomed, you two.
unless you work out *why* he's changed,
since first you wore that wedding ring.
He surely wasn't like that then.
You're not to blame for *anything?*

SWITCH OFF

A man who admires himself when in public?
To me that's a switch-off, a sudden one too.
If, while you're talking, he's lifting a hand up
admiring his manicure rather than you;

or when you're shopping, he's frequently stopping
and using the windows as mirrors instead,
surely it's time for a less vain companion.
Whoever would want such a fellow in bed?
Before long you'd find out – in places like restaurants –
such escorts you'd rather were talking to you
are glancing around for other admirers
(or chatting them up while you've gone to the loo).
Vanity hankers for strong reassurance –
it's never enough to get it from you.
You don't want a plain man, but who'd want a vain man?
I'm always amazed by the women who do!

Moments at Work

A NOTE ON THE OFFICE DRINK-DISPENSER
(with the staff's comments beneath)

THIS DRINK DISPENSER ISN'T WORKING

'It must be someone on the board.'

'Impossible – it can't play golf,
and, anyway, they're all abroad.'

'I know – a week in Martinique.
Fact-finding mission, so they say'.

'What balls! It's just an office jaunt –
a week-long slap-up holiday.'

A made-up story? No, it's true.
At one time staff were far more free
to criticise superiors –
and sometimes most effectively.

OFFICE BONDING DAYS

Those office 'bonding days' I just can't stand;
I've never found false hugs and kisses nice.
And why do firms need days like that at all?
I guess some people find them all a ball.
And if you bomb out, you will pay the price.
I hate all that embracing, shaking hands,
preferring parties in the days of old,
and loathe the paintball games they love, the men,

while preachy speeches make my spirits fall.
At weekends, too. The whole thing leaves me cold.
I cannot face the thought of them again.

THE MOMENT I KNEW I COULDN'T DO IT

A girl in our office – a little bit older –
did something we couldn't.
She'd stand there and 'smoulder'.
So unlike the rest of us – lively and chatty.
The fellows all loved her, she drove them all batty.

She'd gaze at male colleagues, all eyes and dark hair,
and boy, how it mesmerised all the chaps there!
She'd stand there and 'smoulder', creating a bond.
I wondered – can women do that if they're blonde?

Perhaps! I decided to give it a try,
but only to find it put off the first guy.
He looked at me, worried. 'Hey, are you alright?'
You seem to be terribly quiet tonight.

Are you ill, or just tired? Or maybe it's me?
There's something that's wrong, and that's easy to see.'
At once, I was chatty and lively again.
Me 'smoulder'? I couldn't. He'd made that quite plain.

Why is it that only the dark-haired can smoulder?
There are times I still wonder, now that I'm older.
And I warn chatty blondes – you may very soon see
that it won't work at all, as it didn't for me.

A PRESENTATION

A presentation – going well;
they seemed to love the work we'd done.
And – so unusual in a pitch –
presenting it was rather fun.

Smiles and nods all round the table,
all body language going well –
a huge account was almost ours
in what was a stupendous sell.

We could see we'd all but won it,
our art director plainly not.
With horror, I recall his words
that killed our chances on the spot.

Standing up, he braced himself:
'I feel there's something I should say.
There really isn't any reason
this meeting has to last all day.

A child could see these ads are great.
Just look at them! It's clearly true,
and frankly, if you don't agree,
you must be blind – and stupid too!'

The clients looked up in amazement,
and, without a single word,
picked up their notes and left the room,
our final summing up unheard.

We lost the pitch, he lost his job.
and probably his next one too.

It's terrible to see the things
that over-confidence can do.

DAY OF RECKONING

Stuart never bought a round,
although his working colleagues did.
And why? The same old lame excuse.
'My wife allows me just ten quid.

Ten quid a day – her golden rule.
That's not enough to buy a round
and buy the train fare to and fro,
and also use the underground.'

Although he earned the same as us,
this went on for a year or so,
while every day we bought his pint
and listened to his tale of woe.

Fed up with that, we talked to Joe,
the barman that we used to know.
'Today, all drinks on Stuart, please.
We'll make him pay before we go.

Please, could you run a tab for him?
Don't worry, Joe – we'll make him pay.
We know he has a credit card.'
He nodded, smiled and winked. 'Okay!'

Soon Stuart left the company,

and maybe with a sense of shame,
though not much missed, I have to add.
He only had himself to blame.

I sometimes wonder where he went
and where he worked, and what he did –
and whether he's still cadging drinks,
allowed to spend a mere ten quid.

THE PITCH

Damn!
I've left something at home –
today of all days.
How could I?
It's a huge pitch –
and now I'll have to present without it,
a central plank missing
that could take the whole ship down.

I'll find it when I get back,
when it's all too late –
somewhere in the cosy clutter of my kitchen.
That's when I last had it.

I stand up. I start to speak.
I'm struggling without it.
It was the one thing I most needed,
and I left it at home.

My confidence.

THE CHAIRMAN'S WIFE

A gala night – I'd spent a mint
and bought a Valentino dress.
Black, simple, ruched and beautiful.
and pricey too, I must confess.

Long, classic, but with thigh-high slashes,
designed with taste, but also wit.
And, dare I say, with legs like mine
I knew I'd get away with it.

Did wonders for my confidence.
Did wonders for my long, blonde hair.
Did wonders with the fellows too,
with plenty of admirers there.

But not the Chairman's bloody wife.
'A gorgeous dress!', she said that too.
'But black? So very passé, dear.
It's awful how it ages you!'

THE MOMENT SHE BLEW IT

The interview was almost through.
I liked her, thought her face would fit.
She had the skills to join the firm.
And then she went and ruined it.

I took her to the local pub
to introduce her to the team.
She'd fit in perfectly, I thought,
the ideal choice – so it would seem.

'A drink?', I asked. 'No thanks', she said
and smiled at me and shook her head.
'There's something I'd much rather have –
a pack of cigarettes instead!'

Ask someone else to buy your fix?
That's not the wisest thing to do.
And what appalling timing too,
when halfway through an interview!

I bought a pack from the machine
(which most pubs used to have back then)
and had to buy a pack of twenty
since no machines sold packs of ten.

And while I bought it, up in smoke
went all her chances in a trice.
A moment's madness – sadness too,
as otherwise, the girl was nice.

'IT'S COME TO MY KNOWLEDGE....'

That's what our Chairman said to Freddie,
and Freddie laughed. 'Of course, I'm not!
I'm way past practising – I'm perfect!'
The Chairman fired him on the spot.

That often happened in the sixties –
we lost terrific colleagues then,
the word 'gay' years and years away,
when bosses feared (or fired) such men.

And women too, though they were safer.
Not many would admit the fact,
at least not in their place of work
without a risk of being sacked.

And if the firm detected it
while giving you an interview,
you wouldn't get the job at all,
or else were much less likely to.

Laws against discrimination?
They didn't come for many years,
and far too late for friends like Freddie
and several other of my peers.

Freddie flew to San Francisco –
the kindest, funniest of men,
and sadder still, we'd lost a star
and never heard from him again.

Now, so much later, looking round me,
I often miss the things back then,
but then I think of lovely Freddie –
thank God we can't go back again.

And now of course, we have gay marriage
(admittedly too much for some)
and once again I've been reminded
of just how far the world has come.

ROSES

You've travelled north to meet the client –
you're staying in a nice hotel,
and go upstairs to see your room
and walk into a sight from hell.

Red roses – dozens everywhere,
not just one vase – no, several more,
and, worse, you're sure the client bought them,
(and guess what he has bought them for).

Take the fast train back to London?
You can't – a lot depends on this.
Tell yourself that all those roses
are nothing more than kindliness?

Sheer hell! That happened once to me.
An awkward evening lay ahead.
The client asked to see the flowers
when I was going up to bed.

I said 'Tomorrow, if you like,
before I have to catch my train.
Knock on my door at eight o'clock,
and thanks for buying them again.'

Then, six months later, I got married
(no, not to him I'm glad to say),
and what was nice, he sent some roses
the day before our wedding day.

His message? 'May the best man win!
And this time, hope you like the flowers!'
I did, despite the memory
of keeping him at bay for hours.

The best thing you can do in business
is keep your cool and keep your head
when major clients make a pass
and try and get you into bed.

JIM SLATTERY ARRIVES LATE FOR WORK
(a true story)

'Late! *Very late!*' the Chairman barked
when entering the lift with Jim.
'Me too!' replied Jim with a wink,
while smiling gaily up at him.
And now what could the Chairman say?
It saved Jim's bacon, that's for sure.
In fact he heard the Chairman laugh,
alighting at his office floor.
A dash of unexpected wit
can very often save our skin,
and certainly it saved our friend
when very late arriving in.

A PASS

You're at the office Christmas party.
The Chairman makes a pass at you.
Say nothing? Blame it on the booze?
He's clearly had a glass or two.

Worry that your firm rejection
could spoil your prospects later on,
your chances of promotion hindered,
or else in tatters, all but gone?

But contact a solicitor?
Well, that could wreck your chances too,
especially if the Chairman's good.
The staff could start resenting you.

And his defence could be quite simple –
'I blame it on the mistletoe!
A harmless peck as we were dancing.
Is that illegal? Surely, no!'

Forget it? Tell yourself it's Christmas
(unless he tries it on again).
Accept that it can sometimes happen
when people slosh too much champagne?

Keep calm, relax 'til after Christmas,
and play a game of 'Wait and see?'
By then he may have quite forgotten,
or else remember – guiltily.

To blow things out of all proportion
is tempting, but a huge mistake –

moreover, in the silly season,
it's such an easy one to make.

'YOU'RE FIRED!'

You're fired, and why? Because you're hopeless?
That can be very far from true.
You could be good – and someone's jealous,
and itching to get rid of you.

So many times I've seen that happen.
In fact, it's happened twice to me.
Quite often, when we're doing well,
we spark off someone's jealousy.

Just when you think you're shooting upwards,
you're heading down the other way.
Success can mean the exit door
comes that bit closer every day.

Two reasons you can lose a job:
you're hopeless, or the opposite.
And if you're at, or near the top,
that's always the most dangerous bit.

The moment that you're told 'You're fired!'
may not come as a big surprise –
not if you've noticed jealousy
is clearly in a colleague's eyes.

ABOUT TO RESIGN

You drag yourself into the building –
the steps seem steeper every day.
The office clocks are going backwards,
by lunch you long to get away.

The problem is your Project Leader
who joined the firm six months ago.
The whole team's looking for a job,
although she plainly doesn't know.

And now you've gone and landed one –
the deal was settled yesterday.
The Project Leader there is great,
and what is more, there's better pay.

You'll have to work your notice out –
you naturally expected that.
No worries now about the bills
or else the mortgage on your flat.

You go up to the Chairman's office.
You knock. You hear him ask you in.
You're handing him your resignation
and bursting with adrenaline.

How odd – he doesn't seem surprised,
or only just a little bit –
as if he knows what's going on
and probably expected it.

And then you walk back to your office
and see the Project Leader there.

She knows exactly what you've done;
you see that from her icy stare.

You now admit that you've resigned
(and find that part of it quite fun).
She then asks if your colleagues know.
'Oh yes,' you tell her, 'everyone!'

'What? *Everyone* in my department?'
'Of course! We talk – most colleagues do.
We haven't got a problem there.
In fact, the only one is you.'

'And did you say that to the Chairman?'
'Of course not, but I think he guessed.
He seemed to know the team might go,
and, sadly, wished me all the best.'

You've rattled her, that's obvious.
You've gone and rocked her perch a bit.
Resigning isn't always tough.
It can be quite the opposite.

THE CHAIRMAN'S LAST DAY

Colleagues smile politely in corridors
not mentioning my last day.
It is my farewell party tonight,
and I will have to thank them
for the portrait I do not want –

of me, in the chairman's office,
pin-striped, puffed up with the pride I no longer have,
the person I once was,
in the suit I will no longer wear.

I have said goodbye to my chauffeur
and to my car,
and to my name in the car park,
and will now be parked at home in my study,
checking shares while my wife cooks lunch
and the daily hoovers around me
as if I am gathering dust.

I dread what lies ahead,
when the only deadlines
will be when Tesco shuts
and the dog needs to go out,
and meetings will be parties
cooked up by my wife
to save her sanity,
and the only contracts I sign
will be with utility and insurance companies.

I will look up at that portrait
and see who I once was,
and what I have turned into –
a member of the bored.

Already I hear those words:
'I wish you weren't under my feet all day.'

MOTHER OF THE BRAND

We've been in the boardroom since half past three.
I long to be back for my daughter's tea.
I glance at the clock, we're running late,
I will not be home till half past eight.

What do I care about market share
when my daughter cries that I'm not there?
What do I care about Homeblest bread,
or if the brand is ill or dead?

What do I care about market share
when I would love to brush her hair,
then see her safely into bed,
and leave my business notes unread?

I long to be giving my daughter tea,
while my daughter longs to see more of me.
How could she ever understand?
I am the mother of the brand.

THE COPYWRITER'S RESPONSIBILITY

I am the girl who writes the ads,
and one day hopes to earn a bomb.

I am the girl who writes the blurb,
and to whom the words must come.

I am the one who gets the sack,

and quickly if the Muse is dumb.

I am the one who gets the brief
that tells me when the deadline is.
I am the one who answers it,
and tries to give the message fizz.

I am the girl who writes the ads
for TV, press and radio.
I am the girl who writes the stuff
that interrupts your favourite show.

I am the girl who works at night
to try and get the deadline met.
I am the girl who thinks up ads
to post upon the internet.

I am the girl for posters too
and endless, endless tweets on line.
I am the girl who works so late,
I'm often not back home 'til nine.
I am the girl who writes the ads
in hopes they fill the clients' tills.
I am the girl, if they sell well,
who makes them pay such hefty bills.

I am the one who writes the bull;
I am the one responsible.

Metre from 'The responsibility', Peter Appleton

'WHAT DO YOU DO IN LIFE?

If anyone asks that of me, I never say 'Write poetry'.
I know I'd see their faces glazing –
annoying that, but not amazing.
Most think that modern poetry (and very understandably)
is too obtuse, or up its arse, or wallowing in misery.
And so do I, quite frequently;
they have my greatest sympathy.

Few people ever think of wit,
or someone having fun with it.
The concept doesn't cross their minds –
they think of just the opposite.
Keep mum about it, that's my rule,
or else be made to feel a fool.
'Poetry? That's not for me,
I left all that behind at school!'
And what young people *ever* think
that penning poetry is cool?

Much better just to zip my lip
and talk of other things I do,
or things *they* do – that's better still,
and makes them want to talk to you.
I could attempt to make them laugh,
reciting one short comic verse,
but if they didn't laugh at all,
then that could make things even worse.
(In many ways, a poet's life is
always something of a curse.)

It's funny when the things you do
are not what people want to hear.

'Write poetry' is guaranteed
to make most wish you'd disappear.
I guess I've learned to live with it –
as long as book sales do alright –
that fear they have you might recite,
or even worse, bang on all night.
I'm stoic about all of that;
it's every modern poet's plight!

Moments

of

Anger and Regret

MY CONFIRMATION DAY

There at the altar, and red hot with anger,
and now with the bishop's two hands on my head,
instead of the prayer I should have made there,
I fervently wished that the matron was dead.

She'd hidden my shoes before the church service,
returning them only with minutes to go.
'To teach you a lesson for being untidy!
Now *run* to the church, girl!' A half mile or so.

The procession had started its way to the altar.
My parents had panicked to see me not there.
My body was shaking, and visibly sweating.
While running, the veil came away from my hair.

Now, years on, the very thought of Communion
reminds me of murderous ones in my head,
and memories of kneeling without any feeling –
save wishing that harshest of matrons was dead.

TEMPER, TEMPER

You may seldom lose your temper,
but may have lost some friends who do,
amazed to hear their angry words
and sad they then lost touch with you.

You may rarely lose your temper
(and maybe you make that your goal)

or else you're simply born that way,
a tolerant, forgiving soul.

I hardly ever lose my temper,
surprised when other people do,
and also when they say to me
'Not letting go is bad for you.
You need to fire off now and then.
It clears the air, and clears your head.'
Most people would say that these days.
I'd rather bottle up instead.

You may seldom lose your temper,
or ever see that in your friends.
The reason can be very simple –
too often it's where friendship ends.

A MOMENT I'LL NEVER FORGET

A teenaged daughter's temper tantrum –
and pretty much the usual thing;
red-faced, screaming, shouting, swearing,
fed up with me – and everything.

I listened, didn't say a word.
(No chance of getting one word in,
or chance she'd hear it anyway).
At times, we mothers cannot win.

'I'M OFF!' she yelled, and then stormed out,
and slammed the front door as she went.

I sighed, and poured myself a drink –
the taste of it was heaven-sent!

I thought the front door must have cracked –
slammed as it was so forcibly,
but didn't go and check to see,
delighted to have time for me.

Peace and quiet. Well, not exactly –
her words still rang around my ears.
And no one likes to see their child
that angry, and in floods of tears.

One minute later she was back,
and most surprised, I wondered why.
Could this be an apology ?
I'd no doubt find out by and by.

And then she waltzed into the kitchen,
still furious and wild of eye.
And what was it she said to me?
'YOU COULD *AT LEAST* HAVE SAID GOODBYE!'

WHY DO TEENAGERS GET SO ANGRY?

It's often so. Good Lord –
it's more than commonplace in youth
for hormones to be their worst enemy –
that's so frequently the truth!
They lash out, shout with no civility,
and do and say exactly as they please,

and with their teenage rage bring low our spirits,
and sometimes bring us mothers to our knees.
A teenager who's calm? They do exist,
but, my God, they're all too rare, as parents know.
Most teenagers at times become uncouth
and make us parents long for years ago
remembering our children in first youth.
How sharper than a razor's edge it is
to have an angry child within your life!
How tough it is to keep your sanity,
remaining a good mother and good wife!
How draining and how difficult it is
to have an angry child! They'll change one day.
We can but pray that won't be far away.

Metre from King Lear, Act I, Scene IV, William Shakespeare

BOYS

Loads more dirty socks and shirts,
again tossed on the bedroom floor.
Ask *them* to bring the pile downstairs?
They think that's what a mother's for.

Boys? Always snacking, always starving –
and clearing fridges in a wink,
and if they use a plate at all
you'll always find it in the sink.

Boys? Who'd have 'em? Girls are better,
(and, usually, more fragrant too).
What's more, they use the front door mat

a bit more than their brothers do.

Mud and crud from rugby sessions.
And who will brush it up? Just you.
Ask your lazy louts to do it?
Don't waste your breath – they never do!

Neither boys nor girls are easy –
they're all frustrating – that is true.
You have to wait until they're older.
They're mostly nice by thirty-two.

THE MOMENT I WON, AND LOST

Moccasin – now, how's that spelt?
A double 'c' or is it one?
Or is it one 'c', double 's'?
I thought a bet would be quite fun!

'Moccasin', or 'Mocassin'?
I thought I knew, but so did he –
(a chap who sometimes worked for us –
a big name in psychology).

We made a bet, shook hands on it,
and looking back, quite stupidly.
And why? The sum was far too much –
a huge chunk of my salary.

But then, I thought that I was right
in opting for a double 'c'.

The barman fetched a dictionary –
the tension was extraordinary!

Witnesses? Yes, lots of them,
gathering around the bar,
and maybe thinking I was mad
(as copywriters often are).

Wow, huge relief! I'd got it right.
But did he pay a penny piece?
No, not a bean, and furious,
I told him that I'd call the police.

I didn't, though. What good was that?
And this is where the story ends,
except to say that well-known man
lost all respect among his friends.

The story quickly got around,
as stories like that often do.
I wouldn't want a friend like that.
And nor, I'm pretty sure, would you.

IF

If you can keep your cool with children screaming,
and throwing things and lashing out at you,
and slamming doors and fighting with each other
and all the other awful things they do;
if you can watch them yelling in a fury
but swiftly get the family back on track,

achieving that without a loss of temper
and never striking out or yelling back;

if you can take control at all those moments
when things at home are spinning out of hand,
and use a little bit of calm and logic,
and raise your voice, but never once your hand;
if you can bring back peace into the household,
restoring things to where they were before,
and do it firmly, calmly, quickly, fairly –
you're quite a special parent, that's for sure.

If you can set your kids a great example,
the chances are, they'll grow up kind and fair,
and ask for your advice when they are older
while knowing your good judgment will be there.
If you can get through all those awful tantrums
while keeping calm and always in control,
one day your efforts will be well rewarded.
One day you'll know that you've achieved your goal.

If you can talk to children, always kindly,
without a scene or kicking up a fuss,
you're quite a special parent, and a rare one,
a damned sight better than the rest of us.
If you become a mother or a father
your children want to see when you are old,
you've been a very, very special parent;
your heart is what it should be – purest gold.

If you can do all that, I so admire you,
you well deserve the times you'll have ahead,
with your children, afterwards grandchildren,
without the loneliness some old folk dread.

If you forgive in unforgiving moments,
and always do before your race is run,
yours is the earth, and all your children
will always love you 'til your days are done.

Metre from 'If', Rudyard Kipling

ACCUSATION

At Christmas in the supermarket,
I stood in an enormous queue.
And in the trolley right behind
she smiled, a child of one or two.

A lovely smile, a lovely child —
dark-skinned with gorgeous curly hair.
I'd bought some Christmas decorations
and dangled them with time to spare.

She laughed with me, delightedly.
So sweet, I stroked her on the head.
And then her mother turned on me.
I'm still appalled by what she said.

Nothing I could say to her
could calm her down, or call a truce,
I stood accused of not much less
than molestation, child abuse.

The Manager was duly called
and took me for an interview.
Thank God they didn't press a charge,

although the mother asked them to.

Perhaps it's not appropriate
for men to touch a stranger's child,
but tragic that a mother can't
without another going wild.

OUI, JE REGRETTE BEAUCOUP

A thousand books I haven't read,
a load of things not done in bed,
apologies long overdue –
including, maybe, one to you.

A letter that I never sent,
the fortune that I went and spent
on something stupid years ago.
Regrets? A thousand that I know.

Relationships that lasted years
and finally dissolved in tears,
a journey that I didn't do,
and bad decisions – quite a few.

A job I really should have got
and where I could have earned a lot,
my many failings as a mother.
Regrets? There'll always be another.

Regrets – I've hundreds, many, many,
and if you say you haven't any,

I'm sure you love that famous song.
But *no* regrets? And all life long?

Regrets? Of course you have a few,
but surely what you've learned to do
is live with them, get on with it,
and each time learn a little bit?

Not *one* regret? You *must* have some,
especially if you're a Mum!
Not one regret – or two, or three
you didn't do things differently?

IF ONLY I'D BEEN TO A DIFFERENT BOARDING SCHOOL

Freezing corridors in winter.
Freezing classrooms, bathrooms too.
Freezing chapel, twice a day.
And on time off, not much to do.

No TV, radio or films,
two weekends home each term, at most.
No snacks allowed – too many mice –
or chance to make a slice of toast.

And 'sausage slush' served all the time
(thanks to a local factory).
We had to see the slaughterhouse
right after taking GCE.

What's more, at mealtimes where to sit
was difficult, or such a bore –
each day you had to take a card
a prefect gave you at the door.

A5 – where's that? X4 – where's that?
You walked into a milling crowd.
And simply sitting anywhere
was not an option – not allowed.

No married staff, all women too,
who looked like guards from Ravensbruck.
I still recall their faces now –
the ones *not* in my photo book.

Birthday cakes – two pounds, no more,
with slices chopped off if they were,
which ended up in staffroom teas
if loving Mums did not concur.

And horror! Monthly 'bunny' queues,
while pupils waited for STs.
Imagine the embarrassment!
What dragon made us do that? Please!

A hobby club? No room for one.
An art class – yes, but once a week,
and paint was not allowed outside.
An art career? Your chance was bleak.

And loathsome berets on our heads,
each with a toggle on the top.
And, oh, what agony it was
before that toggle got the chop!

All berets still adorned with them
announced that you were not accepted
or liked by people in your form –
a public sign you'd been rejected.

You couldn't chop it off yourself
since everybody else would know,
and sometimes had to wait for months
before they chose its time to go.

No men in sight, except the chap
who came to do the weekly mowing –
the only man we ever saw.
Thank God the grass was always growing.

In fact, not quite the only man –
we saw the local vicar too –
and every Sunday – often twice,
much more than we'd have liked to do.

And yes, there was a yearly dance –
with *boys*! But in an icy hall,
with staff all sitting on the stage,
their eagle eyes upon us all.

A kiss? A grope? Impossible!
The teachers would descend on you,
and promptly drag you off the floor –
well, that's what they were there to do.

One family photo by your bed.
No magazines of any sort.
And bible readings – lots of them,

and few of them were ever short.

Psalms to learn – and off by heart
for talking on the way to pray.
And semolina served up cold
for pudding every single day.

No cosmetics, not allowed,
all hemlines well below the knee,
and no way could we phone up home
if wallowing in misery.

Butter? Coffee? Sundays only,
and biscuits just on parent days -
where families groaned to see us all
in badly chosen (male part) plays.

One play we did was *'Joan of Arc'*.
How many female parts? Just one!
Joan – that's it, the only woman.
To act in *that* was not much fun.

No study for the younger girls –
instead, those draughty corridors,
with radiators never on
and boring lino on the floors.

'Pashes' (crushes) – loads of them!
You had to pick a girl or two,
and also had to make your choice
before your first half-term was through.

Then, even worse, at birthday teas
you had to save your slice of cake

and hand it over to your pash
in secrecy, for heaven's sake!

Lacrosse in biting winter winds,
with jerseys off by halfway through.
'Girls, get running. Now! And faster!
And then the cold won't get to you!'

A gym, but with a rotting floor –
unsafe to do most things in it.
A vaulting horse? Too dangerous.
Instead we had to do 'keep fit'?

And gym parades in underpants
'to check your posture' – yes, that too.
So many things about that school
are unbelievable, but true.

However did I stick it out
until the age of seventeen?
And have I ever once been back?
You're joking! No, I've never been.

And what's its name – my alma mater?
I don't think it is fair to say.
And why? Because it's changed so much –
I've heard it's quite transformed today.
But if you went there, you may guess.
The chances are that you will know,
and recognise the many clues
and what you went through years ago.

A great career ahead of us?
Fulfilment? An exciting life?

Oh, no – I think that most of us
just settled up as someone's wife.

FIRST STEPS

The nanny or the au pair tells us,
and do not guess how sad it is
to hear you've missed those first few steps
with work responsibilities.

Your child might walk again tomorrow,
and once again you won't be there.
You'll have to wait until you're home
and ask the nanny or au pair.

Or, if they caught it on their mobile,
then you can see those first steps too.
But still, it won't be quite the same
as watching them in front of you.

'She walked today – all by herself!'
She walked. You worked. A stab of pain.
The moment's gone, it's now too late –
the chance will never come again.

How many precious things we miss
when stuck at work in offices.
How many moments we regret,
reflecting on how sad it is.

How very painful it can be

to know the nanny or au pair
has witnessed things that we could not,
because, so often, we weren't there.

Moments, thousands of them missed,
that later, can bring so much pain
when children, older, tell us this:
'But, Mummy, you weren't there again.'

Sports days, parties, school events –
so many you could not attend.
You never stop regretting it;
that's something time cannot transcend.

FOR GERRY

I should have come to see you, Gerry,
in those few weeks before you died.
It's not as if I were that busy.
Too late I knew I should have tried.

I should have come to see you, Gerry.
At least, I could have said goodbye.
Perhaps I went and fooled myself
you'd make it, weren't about to die.

I should have come to see you, Gerry,
as I know you'd have come to me.
And now I'll have to live with that
for ever – and regretfully.

I should have come to see you, Gerry,
in those few weeks before you died,
and sat there with you for a while.
Why didn't I? I should have tried.

I should have come to see you, Gerry,
and talked about the times we had.
We could have had a laugh or two,
and now I wouldn't be as sad.

I should have come to see you, Gerry,
I scold myself that I did not.
It's not that I'm too busy now;
time, recently, is what I've got.

I should have come to see you, Gerry.
I hope somehow you know that's true.
I know for sure that *you'd* have tried
if it were me, instead of you.

Moments of Reckoning

FRIENDS TO STAY

It's lovely having friends to stay.
It's also lovely when they go.
I'm sure most people would agree –
at least, most people that I know.

They've been to stay, you've all had fun,
you've entertained them, done your bit,
and suddenly there comes a point
you find you've had enough of it.

You want time for yourself again,
and need a break from cooking too.
(and clearing after every meal)
and other things you've had to do.

You want less noise, a bit of peace,
and much less early morning chat.
You need to simply sit alone
and have a rest from all of that.

You need your kitchen back again.
You need your head back, also true;
you've had enough of planning things
and asking what they'd like to do.

(And if your house is not that big,
the moment that they're on their way
will make it then seem twice the size,
far larger than just yesterday).

How lovely to be on your own,
just you and him, the two of you.

It's smashing when friends come to stay,
and also when they go – so true.

They're in the car, about to leave,
you wave goodbye, and off they drive –
that moment can be just as nice
as greeting them when they arrive!

FEMALE LOGIC

'Darling, do you like this belt,
or does it makes me look too fat?'

'I don't think it's the belt to blame.'

'I can't believe you'd tell me that!'

'Don't want the truth? Don't ask for it.
Quite simple. That's what men would do.'

'We're kinder, we don't tell the truth
if someone doesn't want us to.'

'You should, why lie to anyone?
That's so illogical to me.'

'Why? 'Cos I don't want to hurt them,
and why hurt people needlessly?'

'Women – I don't understand them.'

'And I don't understand you men.
'So should I wear this belt, or not?'

'Oh, *please* don't ask me that again!'

MALE LOGIC

'I'm going now – be back at five.
And *please, please* leave my desk alone.
I want it left the way it is.
You hear me? It's a no-go zone.
I know exactly where things are.
You hear me clearly? Keep away!
Each time you come and tidy up
I have to search for things all day.'

'Oh darling, look at all that trash –
enough to fill a rubbish bin!
I can't stand looking at the mess.'

'Then shut the door, and don't come in!'

YOU'RE ONLY AS HAPPY AS YOUR LEAST HAPPY CHILD

Your least happy child dictates your contentment –
most mothers have heard that, and know that it's true.
The moment we know that a child is unhappy
can bring us down with them, and instantly too.

Now, just when we need to be there more than ever,
precisely the moment we ought to be strong,
we're sinking like they are – perhaps even further,
and then we can't help them, or get it all wrong.

If, while they're struggling, we're doing the same thing
(the opposite, surely, of what we should do),
they'll notice that quickly, and fall even further
and no-one moves forward, not either of you.

And if their unhappiness then lasts for ages
and we plunge alongside, then worse is in store –
they're now left without any mother to turn to,
as all you are doing is depressing them more.

JUST ONE REMARK CAN DO IT

Just one remark can spoil a friendship,
or finish it – and there and then.
However close you've been before,
it's never quite the same again.

Just one remark you can't believe
can all at once quite change your mind
about a friend you never thought
could be so foolish or unkind,
or bigoted, or such a snob.
Before, you'd never noticed it,
but now you have, you will again,
and more than just a little bit.

Just one remark can kill a closeness –
at worst, descending like an axe,
and swiftly slicing through respect
and halting friendship in its tracks.

You ponder over what they said.
They *can't* have said that. Are you sure?
You are – it's sad, you can't go back,
or feel the way you did before.

'COCKEREL-PECKED'

'Cockerel-pecked' – there's no such phrase,
but 'hen-pecked' is a common one:
proof that men don't nag as much
when things around the house aren't done.'

'The fact is, you don't need to nag,
and that is why you rarely do.
You wait until I've done it all,
and then there is no reason to.'

ASDA MOMENT

We've finished our shopping, with two loaded trolleys –
mine is the food one, my husband does drink.
It's always the same when we get to the checkout –
what the assistants immediately think.

They glance at his trolley. 'Oh, having a party?'
'Er, no' says my spouse, and their smile disappears.
And now what to say? They're very embarrassed,
and we are as well. That's happened for years.

GUILT

Another begging letter on the carpet
for those who don't have carpets on the floor,
or even have a shack or tent to live in
and can't imagine what a carpet's for.

I stack it with the others by the toaster
while knowing I should give a whole lot more,
a moment's guilt so many lie unopened
while more appeals keep coming through the door.

I tell myself I pay three standing orders,
while knowing that in truth I could do more,
and then I start to think about our carpets –
the whole lot need replacing, that's for sure.

How awful to care more about the carpets,
and all because I've seen the ones next door.
Too many times we keep up with the Joneses
while millions don't know what a carpet's for.

I sort the leaflets stuffed behind the toaster,
I truly must donate to one or two,
but then go through the bills that lie unopened,
amazed to see the money we'll get through.

Another begging letter on the carpet,
another begging letter through the door.
There's no excuse, I really must do something
for those who don't know what a carpet's for.

'YOU'RE DRINKING TOO MUCH.'

The doctor's told you yet again.
And yes, you know it's true.
You know you have to cut it down,
and do it quickly too.

He asked you what you drank last night.
'Oh, just a glass or two.'
'You're sure it wasn't three or four?'
His eyes bored into you.

You blushed, not knowing what to say.
He studied it – your face.
You longed to grab your bag and run
and get out of the place.

Your doctor's told you yet again,
and last week mine did too.
But can you cut it down or out?
I find it tough – like you.

OVERHEARD AT A PARTY

'Are you with *her* tonight?' she said.
I knew the way her question led.
I listened to how you replied,
and knew just what your words implied.

You didn't know that I could hear,
that I was just a step away.
In fact, it came through loud and clear,
that you and I were yesterday.

'Are you with her tonight?' she said.
'*Tonight* I am', I heard you say.
I heard you kill a marriage dead.
Just three words blew it all away.

A FLOP

A razor-sharp brain, a great speaker,
and about to become a QC.
Superb on his feet in the courtroom –
a flattering partner for me.

A linguist as well – fluent Russian,
good German and Spanish as well.
'That's thanks to TB in my childhood
and tutors for quite a long spell.'

A catch it would seem, perfect escort,
until a week's break in Corfu,

where I swam out to sea to a platform
while reading was all he would do.

Back on the beach he was ploughing
through tomes on industrial law,
with more left behind in our bedroom
which looked just as much of a bore.

Then suddenly, out on that platform,
I was joined by some fabulous guys.
Handsome, amusing and chatty,
with laughter and wit in their eyes.

And then, when he swam out to join us,
he had to be helped to the top.
And, when we left, diving over,
they saw him descend with a flop.

I sensed they were watching his breast-stroke
and noting his skin – lily-white.
Embarrassed, I swam along with him
while longing to get out of sight.

It doesn't say much for my kindness –
I'm the first to admit that is true.
But, sadly, that flop simply killed it,
and showed we were hopeless, we two.

With that, the attraction was over.
It disappeared into the sea.
No matter how brilliant his mind was,
I knew that he wasn't for me.

WAKE-UP MOMENT

'Speed' – a really big thing once.
It kept us girls so Twiggy-thin.
It took away your appetite –
that's what it does, amphetamine.

It speeded everything, did speed.
not just your weight loss, but your brain.
and many doctors doled it out.
But, then, the sixties *were* insane.

You thought like lightning, rarely slept.
In fact, you hardly went to bed
(unless there was a fellow there).
If not, you went to clubs instead.

Speed made everything so speedy.
We girls did everything so fast.
We'd get to work at nine o'clock,
an hour's work done by quarter past.

From smashing, speed then turned to shocking
when one day I got on a train,
and then, in front of someone there,
I popped another pill again.

'What's that?' he asked. 'Amphetamine?'
I smiled, and duly swallowed it.
'That's ageing you,' the fellow said.
'Each time you pop, you age a bit.'

He told me, 'I'm a pharmacist.
I've studied the effects of speed,

and know the harm that it can do –
the *last* thing that you youngsters need.

You'll put on years,' he said to me.
'It speeds the ageing process too.
You're lovely now, but that won't last.
I'd stop right now, if I were you.'

I did. That pill, the very last.
I chucked the rest at Berkhamsted.
If not, I think the likelihood
is now I would be long-since dead.

YOU KNEW, DEEP DOWN...

The place – a favourite beauty spot,
a place you used to meet a lot.
He asked you to be there at two.
'Today, I need to talk to you.'

He told you it was the end that day.
You didn't watch him drive away.
There were no final words from you.
No point. Whatever could you say?

And stunned, you sat there in your car
and listened to the pounding rain.
The sky was crying, so were you –
you knew you'd never meet again.

You knew, deep down, the end was near.
You guessed that he would choose his wife.
You knew it was a tangled mess,
and now he's axed you from his life.

You could not see the way ahead –
your tears, the rain, you couldn't drive.
And for the first time in your life
you wished that you were not alive.

Moments of Depression

THE BLACK DOG

The black dog's back, and won't go out.
He follows me – and everywhere;
and slumps across me in my bed.
The weight of him – it pins me there.

The look of him is terrible.
So sad, downcast is his expression.
I cannot stand those mournful eyes.
Away, black dog – my black depression!

I scold him, tell him 'Go for walkies!';
But will he budge himself? Oh, no!
I'll have to wait 'til he decides
exactly when he wants to go.

Black dogs always own their owners.
What's more, they don't shift easily.
You're on *their* lead, they're not on yours,
and that's the biggest misery.

SHAME ON ME

This week, I felt a bit depressed –
I guess, at times, most people do,
and simply go through bouts of gloom
with very little reason to.

And then I saw the two of them –
a mother with her little boy,

and both with white sticks, darkened glasses,
yet both of them with smiles of joy.

The two were walking down our street,
and talking gaily to each other,
and laughing as they tapped along –
the toddler blind, just like his mother.

I felt ashamed to be depressed,
and also hugely guilty too.
How could I ever feel like that
when walking right beside those two?

AN INSTANT LIFT

Prozac lifts depression,
but flowers work better still.
It's good to keep some flowers
upon the windowsill.

A single bloom can comfort.
One golden daffodil
can lift one's mood in moments,
much faster than a pill.

I come down in the morning –
a flower above the sink
soon starts to lift my spirits,
and sometimes in a wink.

I start to boil the kettle

to make a cup of tea,
and every single morning
a flower smiles back at me.

No medic would prescribe that.
I would. I know a flower
can have a healing magic,
a special soothing power.

An instant lift, a flower,
when all is gloom and doom,
and greatly recommended
when entering a room.

Especially in the morning,
or when the day is grey –
one bloom, one spot of colour
can chase the blues away.

PSYCHIATRISTS

They feel the need to heal themselves –
and do in every session –
and I think that is often why
they enter the profession.

They have a problem lurking there
which started in their youth,
and feel the need to heal themselves.
I'm sure that is the truth.

When I was younger, twenty-two,
my boyfriend was a shrink –
I had to rock the chap to sleep
and never got a wink.

His demons dominated him,
especially at night,
but in the day, they went away –
he seemed to do alright.

We didn't last; his job did though,
he's still a shrink today,
and people say he's doing well
and earning splendid pay.

Your problems work a treat on theirs:
it puts them in perspective,
and helps the healing process too –
I think that's their objective.

I think 'physician, heal thyself '
is often what they think,
and most succeed and pretty well.
I should have been a shrink.

SAD

A lightbox – what a super present!
They say it works for those with SAD.
A Christmas present from my daughter,
who knows that grey days drive me mad.

But then I lost the bloody leaflet
that told the user what to do,
and how to get the thing to work –
so now I'm sad about that too.

SPRING AT LAST

Season of hope, rebirth, new happiness,
with daffodils and snowdrops once again,
and gone at last, that wintry wilderness,
and mourning plants you've lost to frost and rain.
Season of fresh hope and new ambition,
with dreams of what to plant and what to do,
while picturing a gradual transition
as spring arrives and skies return to blue.
You step outside, you wander round the lawn,
your spirits lift, your garden is reborn.
Quite suddenly it soars – your disposition.

With buds now opening up before your eyes,
you feel a surge within your mental state
and do not trouble friends with winter sighs
or look within yourself and curse your fate.
Instead, you dream and plan what you'll be growing
in weeks to come now that the frost has gone,
and all the seeds you'll very soon be sowing –
at last empowered to smile, and carry on.
So long in coming, spring is here at last,
and even though the sky is overcast,
the first new signs of life, at last, are showing.

Age Moments

THE HOUSE EXTENSION

She didn't really need a new extension.
In truth, she needed something else to do,
and now it's been a year of huge disruption
and still the job is only halfway through.

What's more, the builders frequently go missing.
'They've gone to Spain – again – on holiday.
But *I* suspect they're building someone's house there,
and goodness knows how long they'll be away.'

The RSJ is in, but clearly crooked.
The wiring isn't finished, scary too.
The electrician's now switched off his mobile,
and when will he be back? She's not a clue.

Everything is filthy and dust-coated,
and worse, the dust has also gone upstairs.
They didn't use the dust sheets where they should have.
She told them more than once, but no-one cares.

A classic story when we're getting older
and need a challenge, something else to do.
Especially if our partners are still working
and we're alone a lot – that's often true.

It's then we sometimes wonder what we're doing,
and make our homes the focus of it all,
instead of looking outwards; much, much further
than tarting up the kitchen or the hall.

Beware if that extension isn't needed,
or extra bedroom, or another floor.

Too many of us build ourselves a nightmare,
and wonder what on earth we did it for.

SUDDENLY ONE MONDAY

For years we're busy, buzzy, happy, working,
and then retired, with far, far less to do.
That's if we haven't planned and found some challenge,
or never made the time to think things through.

The days ahead can yawn without a project,
with tasks that only take an hour or two
and rarely bring the feeling of fulfilment
as working in a team once used to do.

It's nice to have the time for things like hobbies
and seeing friends and having them to stay,
but less so, if in truth we're simply struggling
with what to do, or how to fill the day.

Retirement can be guilt without a passion –
a stab that says we should be doing more
than sort things out or send a load of emails,
or lose ourselves in yet another chore.

For some, too many, it's about escaping
and spending money we can ill afford
on holidays and trips to distant places,
because, at home, alas, we're often bored.

For others, it's a lot of entertaining,

and making that a time-consuming task,
with recipes they've never tried beforehand,
and working out exactly whom to ask.

And many people start to do the house up
(although, in truth, it looked quite good before),
or move to somewhere else that needs restoring,
to keep them busy for a year or more.

Of course, in lots of ways we're hugely lucky
not to have to work – and every day,
but still, without a focus or ambition,
it never (or it rarely) feels that way.

Retirement can be tough without a passion.
And if we didn't nurture one in youth,
we often end up floating, muddling through it,
while hating facing up to that harsh truth.

At worst, we're cursed with far too many moments
of looking back and often feeling sad
that all the days and years that lie in waiting
won't be as fun as former ones we had.

THE OTHER SIDE OF THE COIN

No alarm clock, no commuting,
not stuck in traffic every day,
no long, long meetings wondering
at what point you can get away.

Weekdays yours – not someone else's,
and, better still, no Sunday blues,
with thoughts of Monday often looming
above the headlines in the news.

The chance to stay up late at night
and entertain on weekdays too,
without the guilt you used to have
with deadlines hanging over you.

No problems now with what to wear
or planning different clothes each day.
Now, if you want to, stick to jeans
and chuck the office suits away.

What's more you're good at what you did,
so why not do it, since you're free?
It might not be impossible
to start up your own company.

The time, perhaps, to learn a sport,
or take up sculpting, paint a bit.
If that that is what appeals to us,
who cares we're not much good at it?

No dreary clients, time for friends,
and fun with them, you've saved for it.
Retired? Oh yes, but not from life.
In fact, it's just the opposite.

You think of all those years behind –
the freedoms that you often missed.
If ever there's a time, it's now
to *grab* them – be an optimist!

ROSE-TINTED GLASSES

Now, looking back, reflecting on past decades
and all the many times that I've been through,
I think the toughest time is getting older –
perhaps the hardest thing we ever do.
But then, we tend to wear rose-tinted glasses
when looking back, reflecting down the years,
not dwelling on the bad or truly sad times
and all the things that ended up in tears.
Today, I think I'll buy rose-tinted glasses –
perhaps I'd look ahead more happily.
What madness looking backwards through pink lenses
and not ahead as optimistically!

'KEEPING BUSY, ARE YOU?'

'Keeping busy, are you?'
A phrase I've come to hate.
And, what's so annoying,
I'm often asked, of late.

No younger person asks that –
it's pensioners who do,
and then you have to wonder
if they are busy too.

The worst thing you can tell them
is 'Yes! Run off my feet!'
and then expand on deadlines
if they have none to meet.

'Yup,' you smile, 'quite busy!'
but don't expand on what.
Most folk won't want to hear it
if they've not done a lot.

And if you aren't that busy,
there's nothing much to say.
Who wants to know that ironing
took up all yesterday?

There's no good way to answer.
These days, I rarely do.
It's best to nod and smile back,
and promptly ask, 'And you?'

AUTUMN YEARS

Season of depth, new-found contentedness,
close bosom friend of many women now,
conspiring with them how to worry less
about the tiny crow's feet on the brow,
and how to fill the days with merry laughter,
and fill more nights with friends around to sup,
and care much less about the morning after,
and wait till then to do the washing up.

Season of calm, and new-found sisterhood,
no enemy of any woman now,
no lies, betrayals, no conspiracies,
no other woman hissing 'Bloody cow'!

THE MIRROR

'Gosh! *That* much on a facelift?
You must be off your head.
Think of all the great things
that we could do instead!

'I just can't face the mirror –
I hate what's looking back.
Everything is dropping,
or else it's going slack.'

'I think you're still attractive,
I like the face I see.
And isn't it sufficient
that you look good to *me*?'

'Well, no, perhaps it should be.
It's confidence, I guess –
how *other* people see me.'

'And me? I matter less?'

LOOKING AT FACES

Often a woman who thinks no-one's looking
wears an expression ineffably sad –
somehow worn down, as if disappointed.
What kind of life has the poor woman had?

She's lost in her thoughts, and thinks no-one's looking.

She looks disappointed, and why can that be?
Promises broken? A humdrum existence?
No difference ahead, or not one she can see?

I watch for a moment and wonder what's happened
to wear an expression that sad on her face,
one that's so different from women much younger.
Why do I find that's so often the case?

Quite often a man who thinks no-one's looking
seems tired and exhausted, but rarely depressed.
Their faces don't wear the same disillusion –
merely the signs they could do with a rest.

Are men's lives so different?
More fun, more fulfilling?
Less humdrum? Less weighed down?
And less duty-bound?
I quite often ponder whenever I wander
and study the faces of women around.

MOMENTS IN A WHEELCHAIR

You notice the potholes and manholes,
and horror, the stretches of cobbles.
You watch out for cracks in the pavement –
and dread them, the subsequent wobbles.

You notice all angles and kerb sides,
and watch out for steps and their height,
and notice the faces that pass you

and how they react to your plight.
You know you won't fall over forwards –
you can't if your straps are in place,
unless you've forgotten to lock them,
in which case, you'll fall on your face.

You notice who smiles and who doesn't,
and people who soon look away,
afraid that a smile suggests pity
when the truth is, a smile makes your day.

Some glance, then they look at your carer,
and wonder if you are his wife.
And sometimes you see people thinking
'Poor bugger, she's ruined his life'.

He pushes the trolley at Waitrose,
you paddle, as best as you can.
He shunts you in front, but so slowly,
and you see them all thinking 'Poor man'.

You loathe all the planning and plotting
that goes into journeys abroad –
the ramps and the walkways, if any,
and the nightmare of getting aboard.

And you notice that people resent it –
the measures now taken for you.
How much has gone on to their tickets
to get the disabled on too?

And you notice, so fast, if disabled,
how often you long for a pee
and find that DISABLED is locked up,

and nobody there has a key.
You notice, if stuck in a wheelchair,
a hundred things other folk won't –
like people who ask why you're in one;
that's nice – the majority don't.

At times it's more safe to pull backwards.
(On steep kerbs, it's safer by far.)
But you don't dare advise who is pushing,
they're sufficiently kind as they are.

And you notice the truth in that cliché;
they talk to your carer, not you.
'Would she like?' is a phrase I've heard often.
They think if you're lame, you're dumb too.

Folk say that you're chatty and upbeat,
that you talk with a laugh in your voice.
You have to, or else you'd be friendless.
Quite frankly, you have little choice.

One day, I'll be out of this wheelchair,
but some things I won't leave behind –
the memories of life trapped within one.
Here's hoping they make me more kind.

INVISIBLE

At twenty, I could turn a head
whenever walking down the street.
In fact, I turned a dozen heads.
It's true, I promise, not conceit.

At thirty, walking down the street
I turned a head, or two, or three.
And workmen often downed their tools
to take a closer look at me.

At forty, walking down the street
some turned their heads, then looked away.
They rarely eyed me up and down,
and just continued on their way.

At fifty, walking down the street
they never saw me pass at all.
They simply walked and stared ahead,
expressions blank, just like a wall.

And now I'm well past pension age,
and once again, they stare at me.
The whole world looks me up and down –
my leg is plastered up, you see.

I broke it falling down the stairs,
a rather silly thing to do.
The unexpected bonus is
I'm absolutely back on view.

The whole street looks me up and down,
from toe to top, and top to toe.
It's lovely to be seen again.
It's splendid to be back on show!

Final Moments

MY MOTHER'S DEATH

It is not frightening to see her.
She is merely a vase from which the flowers have been taken.
We, her children, hold them now.

Not all are beautiful.
Some are as spiky as teasels,
as thorny as brambles,
as barbed as holly.
Others sting like nettles.
But I don't notice those.

I look at the best of my bouquet –
buttercups held under our chins –
'Yes, you love butter!'
Dandelion seeds blown and scattered –
'She loves me, she loves me not'.
Daisy chains made in the garden.
'Keep still, while I put them on!'
Walks in woods when the foxgloves
were taller than we were.
'Shall I tell you a ghost story?'

Dells ablaze with bluebells –
'Look – like the sea!'
Lilies on the lake on our summer holidays –
'Watch out – you'll get your oars tangled!'
Flowers around our plates on every birthday,
and posies of violets picked for Mother's Day.

She has handed them back to us.
I have enough to look at for the rest of my life.

THE FUNERAL

'Jim Wilson had the finest mind,
and best of all, was truly kind.
Our feelings go to Jane, his wife,
and all those here who shared his life.
Jim was generous, warm and witty
and so successful in the City.
What's more, a legend it is said
when on the board of RTZ
as such a sympathetic boss,
if anybody made a loss.
Jim was caring, Jim was funny,
and dedicated all his money
to helping people out in life.
Our feelings go to Jane, his wife.'

'Psst! Is this funeral for Jim?
It doesn't sound a bit like him!
And *I* should know – I'm Jane, his wife.
It sounds like quite another life!'

THE PLAY

I see you, you do not see me,
I'm right behind you in row C.
I watch you, as you watch the play,
I'm deaf to what the actors say.

I used to love your cloud of hair,
so thick, so wild in wind, corn-fair.

But now your scalp is shiny red
and sweat beads glisten on your head.

Your collar is too tight on you,
a larger size is overdue.
You're bald, seem shorter, overweight.
And flustered from arriving late.

Is that your wife with sprigs of grey?
I guess I have a few today.
If we meet later, what to say —
how much we both enjoyed the play?

You drop the programme on the floor
and find retrieving it a chore.
Your waistband stops you reaching down.
You shuffle, fidget, scratch and frown.

Can it be true? Can it be true?
The man in front of me is you?
I marvel now at all the tears
that ended almost twenty years.

You whisper something to your wife.
I'm glad I have another life.
The curtains open for Act Two
and close, at last, on me and you.

A HAPPY ENDING

Please, when I go, no eulogy
or solemn words in praise of me.